Spring Harvest Bible Workbook

PSALMS

Cries from the heart

Joseph Steinberg

D1113827

Series editor for Bible workbooks – Ian Coffey

Authentic

SPRING HARVEST

Equipping the Church for action

12 11 10 09 08 07 06 7 6 5 4 3 2 1

First published in 2006 by Spring Harvest Publishing Division and Authentic Media
9 Holdom Avenue, Bletchley, Milton Keynes, Bucks, MK1 1QR, UK
and 129 Mobilization Drive, Waynesboro, GA 30830-4575, USA

www.authenticmedia.co.uk

Authentic Media is a division of Send the Light Ltd, a company limited by guarantee
(registered charity no. 270162)

British Library Cataloguing in Publication Data

A catalogue record for this book is available from the British Library

ISBN 1-85078-689-5

Typeset by Spring Harvest
Cover design by fourninezero design
Print management by Adare Carwin
Printed by J. H. Haynes & Co. Ltd., Sparkford

For my children, Jessica, Benjamin and Emily, for whom my heart cries out to God in thankfulness. May the Lord always keep you like trees planted by streams of water which yield their fruit in season and whose leaves never wither (Ps. 1:3).

CONTENTS

About this book   5

Introduction to the Psalms   7

Session 1: Crying out for happiness   8

Session 2: Crying out for committed love   12

Session 3: Crying out for salvation   17

Session 4: Crying out in suffering   22

Session 5: Crying out for God's presence   28

Session 6: Crying out for comfort   33

Session 7: Crying out for forgiveness   38

Session 8: Crying out in thanks and praise   43

Leaders' Guide

Introduction   48

Session 1: Notes   52

Session 2: Notes   54

Session 3: Notes   56

Session 4: Notes   58

Session 5: Notes   59

Session 6: Notes   61

Session 7: Notes   62

Session 8: Notes   64

ABOUT THIS BOOK

This workbook is written primarily for use in a group situation, but can easily be used by individuals who want to study the heart cries of the psalms. It can be used in a variety of contexts, so it is perhaps helpful to spell out the assumptions that we have made about the groups that will use it. These can have a variety of names – home groups, Bible study groups, cell groups – we've used housegroup as the generic term.

▶ The emphasis of the studies will be on the application of the Bible. Group members will not just learn facts, but will be encouraged to think: 'How does this apply to me? What change does it require of me? What incidents or situations in my life is this relevant to?'

▶ Housegroups can encourage honesty and make space for questions and doubts. The aim of the studies is not to find the 'right answer', but to help members understand the Bible by working through the questions. The Christian faith throws up paradoxes. Events in people's lives may make particular verses difficult to understand. The housegroup should be a safe place to express these concerns.

▶ Housegroups can give opportunities for deep friendships to develop. Group members will be encouraged to talk about their experiences, feelings, questions, hopes and fears. They will be able to offer one another pastoral support and to get involved in each other's lives.

▶ There is a difference between being a collection of individuals who happen to meet together every Wednesday and being an effective group who bounce ideas off each other, spark inspiration and creativity and pool their talents and resources to create solutions together and whose whole is definitely greater than the sum of its parts. The process of working through these studies will encourage healthy group dynamics.

Space is given for you to write answers, comments, questions and thoughts. This book will not tell you what to think, but will help you to discover the truth of God's word through thinking, discussing, praying and listening.

FOR GROUP MEMBERS

▶ You will get more out of the study if you spend some time during the week reading the passage and thinking about the questions. Make a note of anything you don't understand.

▶ Pray that God will help you to understand the passage and show you how to apply it. Pray for other members in the group too, that they will find the study helpful.

▶ Be willing to take part in the discussions. The leader of the group is not there as an expert with all the answers. They will want everyone to get involved and share their thoughts and opinions.

▶ However, don't dominate the group! If you are aware that you are saying a lot, make space for others to contribute. Be sensitive to other group members and aim to be encouraging. If you disagree with someone, say so but without putting down their contribution.

FOR INDIVIDUALS

▶ Although this book is written with a group in mind, it can also be easily used by individuals. You obviously won't be able to do the group activities suggested, but you can consider how you would answer the questions and write your thoughts in the space provided.

▶ You may find it helpful to talk to a prayer partner about what you have learnt, and ask them to pray for you as you try and apply what you are learning to your life.

▶ The New International Version of the text is printed in the book. If you usually use a different version, then read from your own Bible as well.

INTRODUCTION

When I became a follower of Jesus life was difficult. I was a teenager in a Jewish home who had come to believe Jesus is the promised Messiah. To say my parents were unhappy is an understatement. My relationship with my father was ruined, my mother didn't understand this 'phase I was going through' and I found little sympathy among my siblings at that time. I was forbidden to go to church and I had to hide my Bible in a slit in my mattress in order to keep it from being thrown away.

During those days there were many times in which I felt alone, misunderstood, different even from my Christian friends who seemed to have it so easy, and sometimes I felt depressed. My faith in Jesus may not have made my life 'apple pie in the sky by and by' but one thing was for certain – I knew God was real and on my side.

What does any of this have to do with the book of Psalms? The psalms helped sustain me during those difficult years at home. I spent many a night using chapters from the psalms as the basis for my heart cries to God. They brought me comfort as I cried out to a God who was there for my ancestors and now for me. The words of the poets, hymn writers and sages of this book became my words to the Almighty.

Of course, not all my days were difficult – some of the most exhilarating memories of my life are from those first years of my newfound faith. And even during moments of great emotional height, again I found myself in the psalms – using the words there to help guide my thanking, praising and worshipping God for his love, faithfulness and understanding.

This workbook only covers a very small amount of the vast poetry, wisdom and hymnody of the psalms. But I hope that in using it, you will discover or rediscover the enormous amount of help and guidance God has given us in the psalms. Help for crying out to an infinitely loving and compassionate Creator who knows us to the depths of our being, loves to hear our heart cries to him and ultimately comes to our aid.

Finally, it is my prayer that you will grow deeper in the ability to express yourself to God and hear his heart cries for you. And may you find, as I have, the Lord to be the one on whom you can 'cast your cares... because he will sustain you' (Ps. 55:22).

CRYING OUT FOR HAPPINESS

Aim: To discover the source of true happiness

Do a Google internet search with the words 'happiness is' and you will find a plethora of offerings. Just a selection found under the letter C tells us that happiness is: cats, cream pies, camping, cars, cooking, crayons, carving, coriander and a choice. In fact, Google came up with almost 34 million pages of happiness.

Perhaps Google didn't get it all wrong. According to Psalm 1, happiness is a choice. What kind of choice?

Read the passage together

Blessed is the man
who does not walk in the counsel of the wicked
or stand in the way of sinners
or sit in the seat of mockers.
But his delight is in the law of the Lord,
and on his law he meditates day and night.
He is like a tree planted by streams of water,
which yields its fruit in season and whose leaf does not wither.
Whatever he does prospers.

Not so the wicked!
They are like chaff that the wind blows away.
Therefore the wicked will not stand in the judgment,
nor sinners in the assembly of the righteous.
For the Lord watches over the way of the righteous,
but the way of the wicked will perish.

Psalm 1:1-6

TO SET THE SCENE

Ask everyone to write one hobby or activity that makes them happy onto a slip of paper. Collect the slips and then give everyone one each and ask them to match the hobby with the right person. Then ask people to say why they enjoy the hobby and what they get out of it.

DID YOU KNOW?

Psalm 1 is considered by many commentators to be the 'psalm of psalms.' It has been called 'the preface psalm', 'the doorkeeper' of the psalms, and 'the introductory psalm.' Many believe all of the psalms can be summed up in this first psalm.

Most psalms can be classed as either praise, prayer or prophetic, but Psalm 1 is classed as a wisdom psalm – an instructive psalm more akin to the book of Proverbs than what we would see as a traditional psalm.

The Westminster Catechism states, 'Man's chief end is to glorify God and enjoy him forever.' Psalm 1 is concerned with making sure we know God and joyfully experience him.

There are many parallels between Psalm 1 and Jesus' Sermon on the Mount – both begin with 'blessed', which is the same word in the Bible as 'happy.'

---

1. This psalm is concerned with helping us discover happiness in all its fullness. What a surprise that the first verse starts with a negative to the power of three! Can you identify what 'walking, standing and sitting' look like for Christians today? Can you see a process of movement away from God in these word pictures? If so, how?

2. Verse 2 tells us that by 'delighting' in God's law and meditating on it 'day and night' we will find true happiness. What do you consider to be 'God's law' for us?

APPLY THIS TO

MY CHURCH

3. What do you think is meant by 'delighting' and 'meditating'? Is it something others in your church do? How can we encourage each other in this?

ENGAGING WITH THE WORLD

4. In verses 4–5 the psalmist compares the wicked to chaff – rootless, useless seed coverings that get blown away. Think of people you know who may be better off than you... what do their lives seem rooted in? How content are they? How different are your roots?

HOW DOES THIS APPLY TO ME

5. In the Hebrew, the word translated 'watches' here is more about God knowing and choosing your way, leading you into his way and ordering your path. How does it make you feel to know God goes with you on the journey he has set for you?

6. How can you encourage those around you to spend more time understanding what it means to love God's law and put it into practice? What does that look like? What would encourage you?

Read the Beatitudes in Matthew 5:1–16

WHAT DOES THE BIBLE SAY?

7. What have you discovered from Psalm 1 that changes the way you understand Jesus' teaching in Matthew 5:1–12? Are there verses that stand out for you that at first glance would appear the opposite to happy, but now have a deeper meaning?

8. Matthew 5:13–16 reveals God's desire that our happiness be contagious. By using the images of salt and light, how much would you say you affect those around you? Can they taste your faith or are you without flavour? Are you so bright they hide their eyes? Is your happiness contagious?

WORSHIP

In verse three of this passage the psalmist uses the imagery of a beautiful fruitful tree planted by streams of water. Close your eyes and imagine yourself as a tree. What kind of tree are you? How green are your leaves? What kind of fruit are you bearing? How much? Now survey your roots. Do they go down deep or are they closer to the surface? Will they sustain you through the terrible winds of fierce storms? Do they go deep enough to get water during droughts?

Take a minute to offer yourself as a tree to God the Gardener. Hear his still small voice in your heart as he seeks to encourage you closer towards him as both the water and light of life.

Get in groups of two and share what you saw of your tree. Encourage one another in what you feel you are doing right to cultivate your tree and what you may be able to do better. Finally, pray for one another in your pairs – that God would help you as you seek to know him and experience his happiness.

DURING THE WEEK

Think back to the start of this study, when you wrote down an activity or hobby that makes you happy. Focus on one person you know who does not yet have the same relationship with God that you have. Take back the slip of paper you used at the beginning and write their first name on the blank side. Begin to pray for that person and for yourself – that you both would have a God-appointed opportunity for you to be able to share something of your happiness and relationship with God in way that will be meaningful to them. Keep praying for them and seeking ways to be salt and light to them, that they too will experience God's happiness in all its fullness.

CRYING OUT FOR COMMITTED LOVE

Aim: To gain a deeper sense of God's intimate, unfailing love for us

TO SET THE SCENE

Take a stopwatch and give the group three minutes to list everything they know about a well-known person. The person can be a celebrity, a political leader or even your own minister. Have one group member try to jot it all down as you go.

Take a few minutes to reflect on what you knew about the person. Was it more or less than you expected? How would that person feel about how much you knew and how accurate your knowledge was? Would they feel the group's summing-up was accurate? How would they feel about any of the motives or actions ascribed to them? Do you think they would feel they are always treated fairly?

Finally, take a moment to reflect on how well your life would fare under the same exercise. Perhaps only those closest to you would know much about you without the scrutiny of the press. But what about the feelings and motives behind your life's actions? Do you feel you would always be understood and fairly represented by those who spoke or write about you?

Read the passage together

Sing joyfully to the Lᴏʀᴅ, you righteous;
it is fitting for the upright to praise him.
Praise the Lᴏʀᴅ with the harp;
make music to him on the ten-stringed lyre.
Sing to him a new song;
play skillfully, and shout for joy.

For the word of the Lᴏʀᴅ is right and true;
he is faithful in all he does.
The Lᴏʀᴅ loves righteousness and justice;
the earth is full of his unfailing love.

By the word of the LORD were the heavens made,
their starry host by the breath of his mouth.
He gathers the waters of the sea into jars;
he puts the deep into storehouses.
Let all the earth fear the LORD;
let all the people of the world revere him.

For he spoke, and it came to be;
he commanded, and it stood firm.
The LORD foils the plans of the nations;
he thwarts the purposes of the peoples.
But the plans of the LORD stand firm forever,
the purposes of his heart through all generations.

Blessed is the nation whose God is the LORD,
the people he chose for his inheritance.
From heaven the LORD looks down
and sees all mankind;
From his dwelling place he watches
all who live on earth-
He who forms the hearts of all,
who considers everything they do.
No king is saved by the size of his army;
no warrior escapes by his great strength.
A horse is a vain hope for deliverance;
despite all its great strength it cannot save.
But the eyes of the LORD are on those who fear him,
on those whose hope is in his unfailing love,
To deliver them from death
and keep them alive in famine.

We wait in hope for the LORD;
he is our help and our shield.
In him our hearts rejoice,
for we trust in his holy name.
May your unfailing love rest upon us, O LORD,
even as we put our hope in you.

Psalm 33: 1-22

1. This psalm is a psalm of praise and it begins with the command to 'sing joyfully to the Lord!' Get into twos and list why the psalmist starts with such a positive call to worship. What can you learn about God's feelings about us from this passage? Share your discoveries as a group.

2. Verses 4–9 focus in on God's creative word. The thing to note here is not that God spoke everything into existence, but how or with what attitude he did so. What can you see here about how God feels about all he has made? Does this surprise you? Does he still feels this way?

3. Verse 8 proclaims that all the earth should fear the Lord. Looking at this verse in context, how would you best define the 'fear of the Lord'? What reasons can you find for the psalmist to say that all people of the world should revere God?

4. While we see all of nature giving glory to God in verse 8, verses 10–12 speak of humanity's deliberate disobedience to God's will. According to these verses, how long does it take for God's will to be finally accomplished in our lives? What does this say about God's commitment to us as our Creator and Lord of all?

Read Romans 8:28-38

5. According to Romans 8, how does God feel about us? How does this passage make you feel about God's will and commitment to you? Why? Can you note the parallels between what Paul is writing here and what the psalmist wrote in Psalm 33?

6. How do Psalm 33 and Romans 8:28-39 help you feel about the future of the church? What about the future of the world God has created? What practical ways can the group think of to participate in God's will for the church better?

7. In verses 13-19 the psalmist shows us the world through God's eyes. How does Romans 8:28-30 help us understand how completely God sees and knows us? Contrast what God knows about the human heart with Jeremiah 17:9, which says: 'The heart is deceitful above all things and beyond cure. Who can understand it?'

8. Verses 16-17 contrast the saving power of great human effort with the saving power of God in verses 18-19. What is it that God is looking for in his people?

9. Read Galatians 5:22-23 and contrast that reading with Psalm 33:20-21. How does what you have learned about God's ever-loving commitment to you make you feel about the reasons why we should be seeing more and more of the fruit of the Spirit in our daily lives?

10. Psalm 33 ends with a statement of hope. Why can the psalmist end with such a statement of resting in God? What is the psalmist hoping in? How is that demonstrated in what we know of the way God works in our lives?

WORSHIP

At the beginning we thought about how well we knew a famous person. Now take a few minutes to imagine yourself as a famous person – under the scrutiny of the press and paparazzi. See all the flashes of the press at key moments in your life. How would you feel about everyone knowing the ins and outs of your life?

Now reflect on Psalm 33 and the fact that God does know the ins and out of your personal life – even the inner thoughts of your heart. How does that make you feel? Remember his knowledge of you in the light of his loving-kindess.

Take a moment to quietly thank God quietly for his everlasting love and mercy. Thank him for his commitment to you – to deliver you to himself. Ask him to help you trust and hope in him more. Ask the Spirit to sow more of his fruit in your life.

DURING THE WEEK

Take a few minutes each day to read a headline about a person. After reading, pray for them. Lift them before the God who truly knows them and ask for him to reveal more of himself and his loving-kindness to them. Close your prayer time with the last verse of this psalm, 'May your unfailing love rest upon us, O LORD, even as we put our hope in you.'

CRYING OUT FOR SALVATION

Aim: To understand the implications of God's salvation

'Trust me' is something we are asked to do from time to time, whether it is a political leader asking for our unswerving commitment or someone close asking us to believe in them. But trust can be quite hard when we so often feel we can do the job better ourselves – especially in terms of our salvation.

Trusting God to save is the main thing that separates Christianity from all the world's other religions. All other religions trust human works to save, while we are called to trust in God's works.

But if we do trust in God and all he has done to save us, the resulting joy will produce a song in our hearts and a word for the world!

> Sing to the LORD a new song;
> sing to the LORD, all the earth.
> Sing to the LORD, praise his name;
> proclaim his salvation day after day.
> Declare his glory among the nations,
> his marvellous deeds among all peoples.
>
> For great is the LORD and most worthy of praise;
> he is to be feared above all gods.
> For all the gods of the nations are idols,
> but the LORD made the heavens.
> Splendour and majesty are before him;
> strength and glory are in his sanctuary.
>
> Ascribe to the LORD, O families of nations,
> ascribe to the LORD glory and strength.
> Ascribe to the LORD the glory due his name;
> bring an offering and come into his courts.
> Worship the LORD in the splendour of his holiness;
> tremble before him, all the earth.

Say among the nations, "The LORD reigns."
The world is firmly established, it cannot be moved;
he will judge the peoples with equity.
Let the heavens rejoice, let the earth be glad;
let the sea resound, and all that is in it;
let the fields be jubilant, and everything in them.
Then all the trees of the forest will sing for joy;
they will sing before the LORD, for he comes,
he comes to judge the earth.
He will judge the world in righteousness
and the peoples in his truth.

Psalm 96

TO SET THE SCENE
You've seen it in films... you know it's crazy... but do it anyway.

Have people team up into pairs. Have one person blindfold the other and then lead them safely around the room. If the weather permits, have a short stroll around the neighbourhood. Once a few minutes have passed, reverse roles and do it again.

At the end, have everyone talk briefly about how they felt entrusting themselves to another for safekeeping. Did you trust one another enough to get through this exercise without peeking?

Read the passage together

DID YOU KNOW?
This psalm is set in the context of 1 Chronicles 16 – in fact it is restated there in verses 23–33. In this passage, David is bringing the Ark of the Covenant into Jerusalem, the former home of the pagan Jebusites he had conquered earlier.

The act of placing the Ark in Jerusalem was akin to making a statement about God's sovereign right to rule the nations. This psalm reflects the heart of that message. God is not Israel's God alone, but he is the Lord God of all creation, who will redeem the world and rule it in his strength and glory.

However, the theme is that of salvation. The Lord God Almighty, Yahweh, is the only God who will judge the earth and its peoples, making all things right. And he is the only God who can save people from that righteous judgement and make them new. The result of such good news is jubilant singing and the declaring of God's goodness and marvellous deeds.

1. If you were asked, 'What is salvation?' how would you answer? If you were asked to answer the same question using all of Psalm 96, what would be your answer?

WHAT DOES SEARCH THE BIBLE SAY?

2. Using verse 1, think about whether your salvation is a one-off act or an ongoing process? Is salvation for individuals alone or is it more global? Read Lamentations 3:22–23. Does this help clarify your thinking? How?

HOW DOES THIS APPLY TO ME

3. In verses 2 and 3 we are called to 'proclaim' God's salvation and 'declare' his glory among the nations. How do we 'proclaim' and 'declare' today? How could you be more effective?

4. Verse 4 tells us that God is both worthy of praise and yet to be feared (revered) above all gods. In light of the salvation God offers, how should we feel about him? Is God your best friend, your Lord, or a disappointed ruler ready to step on you? Does he feel far away, close by, sometimes on holiday? Does he care intimately for you, with a plan for your life, or is he not that bothered?

HOW DOES THIS APPLY TO ME

5. The Hebrew word used for idol in verse 5 means 'useless.' The contrast here is between trusting in idols made by men or trusting in God who made the heavens. List some of the things you find yourself trusting in more than God. How can you trust more in God?

ENGAGING WITH THE WORLD

6. Together, verses 5 and 6 are making an 'exclusive truth claim.' There is only one God: Yahweh. Verses 3, 7 and 11 state that God's salvation is not just for Israel but for all people. Only Yahweh can save the world.

Compare these verses with John 14:6. How does this make you feel about other religions and the salvation

they offer? How can you share God's salvation with those of different faiths?

WHAT DOES SEARCH THE BIBLE SAY?

7. Verses 3, 7 and 11–12 show us that it is God's will for all of creation to know him and declare his praises – from all of nature to all people. Read Romans 8:18–25. Why do you think creation waits and groans for the children of God to be revealed? When this happens, what will it look like?

APPLY THIS TO MY CHURCH

8. A true understanding of all that God has done in saving us should produce worshipfulness and gratitude. Verses 8 and 9 ascribe credit to God for what he has done and show the response we should have in presenting offerings for such a great work. In David's day the offerings were sacrifices of grain and animals. What could we offer God today?

9. Verses 10–13 show us that God's judgement of all will come and it will be fair. How do you feel knowing God will judge all people? Will you be able to withstand God's scrutiny of your life? Will you be judged righteous or guilty? Why?

If we are trusting in his salvation – we know we are righteous; not because of anything we have done, but only because we trust in Jesus who gave his life on our behalf.

WORSHIP

Psalm 96 shows us that salvation is about being made new. It is for all of God's creation – everyone and everything. When experienced it is impossible to keep quiet about, both in worshipping God and in telling others. Only God can work authentic salvation and truly experiencing it produces a deep gratefulness and reverence of him. God's salvation removes the fear and dread of the certain coming judgement and will produce an everlasting joy throughout all of creation. Psalm 96 tells us salvation is for now, for ever and for certain.

With all that in mind, take a few minutes to be quiet and reflect on what salvation means to you. How do you feel God's salvation has affected you? Consider your life; past, present and future. Has it made a difference? What can/will you do to help it make a difference in the lives of others?

Now write down a prayer of thanks and praise to God for his salvation. Try to use your prayer once a day through the coming week to help you remember and reflect on all that God has done and will do for you.

When everybody has finished, end your session by allowing those who wish to read their prayers aloud.

DURING THE WEEK

Make a time each day this week to read Isaiah chapter 12.

The Hebrew word for salvation in this passage is 'Y'shua.' This word was also Jesus' name. In Matthew 1:21 the angel of the Lord appeared to Joseph and told him, 'Mary will give birth to a son, and you are to give him the name Jesus (Y'shua – 'God saves') because he will save his people from their sins.'

After reading Isaiah 12, take a few minutes to thank God for the salvation he has provided for you and ask him to give you someone to share his salvation with that day. Be ready for the opportunity that will arise to be good news to someone else!

CRYING OUT IN SUFFERING

Aim: To discover God's nearness in suffering

'God, where are you in all this?' is something we all feel at one time or another. In fact, the number one question unbelievers have is how can God exist in the light of all the suffering in the world?

We all want to avoid suffering – whether that is illness, the loss of one we love or even our own death. But in Psalm 22, the cry of David is not that suffering should be removed, but that he should feel God's presence near him in his suffering.

Perhaps Psalm 22 can help us find God when we are hurting.

Read the passage together

My God, my God, why have you forsaken me?
Why are you so far from saving me,
so far from the words of my groaning?
O my God, I cry out by day, but you do not answer,
by night, and am not silent.

Yet you are enthroned as the Holy One;
you are the praise of Israel.
In you our fathers put their trust;
they trusted and you delivered them.
They cried to you and were saved;
in you they trusted and were not disappointed.

But I am a worm and not a man,
scorned by men and despised by the people.
All who see me mock me;
they hurl insults, shaking their heads:
"He trusts in the LORD;
let the LORD rescue him.
Let him deliver him,
since he delights in him."

22   SESSION 4

Yet you brought me out of the womb;
you made me trust in you
even at my mother's breast.
From birth I was cast upon you;
from my mother's womb you have been my God.
Do not be far from me,
for trouble is near
and there is no one to help.

Many bulls surround me;
strong bulls of Bashan encircle me.
Roaring lions tearing their prey
open their mouths wide against me.
I am poured out like water,
and all my bones are out of joint.
My heart has turned to wax;
it has melted away within me.
My strength is dried up like a potsherd,
and my tongue sticks to the roof of my mouth;
you lay me in the dust of death.
Dogs have surrounded me;
a band of evil men has encircled me,
they have pierced my hands and my feet.

I can count all my bones;
people stare and gloat over me.
They divide my garments among them
and cast lots for my clothing.

But you, O Lᴏʀᴅ, be not far off;
O my Strength, come quickly to help me.
Deliver my life from the sword,
my precious life from the power of the dogs.
Rescue me from the mouth of the lions;
save me from the horns of the wild oxen.

I will declare your name to my brothers;
in the congregation I will praise you.
You who fear the Lᴏʀᴅ, praise him!
All you descendants of Jacob, honour him!
Revere him, all you descendants of Israel!
For he has not despised or disdained

the suffering of the afflicted one;
he has not hidden his face from him
but has listened to his cry for help.

From you comes the theme of my praise in the great assembly;
before those who fear you will I fulfil my vows.
The poor will eat and be satisfied;
they who seek the LORD will praise him—
may your hearts live forever!
All the ends of the earth
will remember and turn to the LORD,
and all the families of the nations
will bow down before him,
for dominion belongs to the LORD
and he rules over the nations.

All the rich of the earth will feast and worship;
all who go down to the dust will kneel before him—
those who cannot keep themselves alive.
Posterity will serve him;
future generations will be told about the Lord.
They will proclaim his righteousness
to a people yet unborn—
for he has done it.

Psalm 22:1-31

TO SET THE SCENE

As a group, think of those you know who are suffering – perhaps even facing death.
If you can, share their stories. Are there those whom you admire for their courage?
Have some struggled more and others less? Contrast their experiences and discuss
what you think have made them different. Discuss what you think you would do if
you were in similar circumstances.

DID YOU KNOW?

Psalm 22 describes an instance in the life of David where he was suffering extreme agony. Although we don't know which experience he is writing about, we know these words express a real experience for him.

It is remarkable that these words also look like the experience of David's descendant, the man Jesus, the Son of God, when he suffered on the cross.

By thinking about our pain in light of all that Jesus suffered on our behalf, we can appreciate God not only understanding us in our anguish, but also having had the experience of suffering all that we endure – and beyond (see Heb. 4:15; 5:7-10). We can take comfort from being in a relationship with a God who knows us, understands us and is forever on our side.

1. In verses 1–5 the cry of the psalmist is that although he has known God's presence in the past – as have his ancestors – now God is gone. Have you ever experienced a time when you felt God was gone? How did you cope? What helped you rediscover God's presence?

WHAT DOES SEARCH THE BIBLE SAY?

2. Look at verses 6–8. How do you feel when you are scorned or mocked because of your faith? How do you respond? Look at Luke 23:32–34. What can you learn from Jesus about responding to persecution?

3. What thoughts could be seen as David's consolation in verses 9–11?

HOW DOES THIS APPLY TO ME

4. When you are suffering what do you most want? Relief? Help? Consolation? Something else? Whom do you call for help or comfort? What is it that David wants in verse 11?

5. Verses 12–18 paint a picture of the strong closing in on the weak. In verse 15 David seems to be placing the responsibility of his suffering on God. Have you ever felt God put you in the midst of a terrible

trial? How did you feel about God allowing that? What is your perspective on that time now? Why?

6. Do you think David finally came to understand how God's presence was with him, even if he did not feel it? Look at verses 24–26. How do his words in this passage show that? Does that help your perspective on suffering? How?

7. If God is all-powerful, why doesn't he stop suffering? Does it mean he is not all loving? Or is he all loving but not all powerful? What do you think? What can you find in the Bible to support your view?

8. The last section of Psalm 22 (vv 22–31) speaks of a day when all the world's wrongs will be righted and the world will sing praise to God as deliverer, provider and ruler of all. How can keeping a perspective of God as one who hears and delivers help you in the midst of suffering?

GOD SUFFERS FOR US
Compare the words of Psalm 22 with the experience of Jesus on the cross:

- Verse 1 – Matthew 27:46 – Jesus cries out these words
- Verse 2 – Matthew 27:45 – The change from day to night
- Verses 6-8 – Matthew 27:39–44 – People scorn Jesus
- Verse 11 – Matthew 26:56 – Jesus is deserted in his trouble
- Verses 12-14 – Matthew 27:27–31 – Jesus is surrounded by the strong
- Verse 16 – Matthew 27:35 – Jesus' hands and feet are pierced
- Verse 17 – Luke 23:35 – People stare at Jesus
- Verse 18 – John 19:23–24 – The guards gamble for Jesus' clothes
- Verse 31 – John 19:30 – Jesus' final cry parallels the words 'he has done it'

WORSHIP

Read Matthew 27:27–50 as a group. Take time together to reflect on all that Jesus has undergone on our behalf. In prayer, thank God for his salvation through Jesus and for knowing what we humans experience – even the extreme experience of feeling he had been forsaken by God.

DURING THE WEEK

This week remember those you know who are suffering. They may feel low, or that God is far away, or they may be very ill, even in hospital or facing death. Pray for them each day and try to visit them once this week, if you can. Don't feel you have to say anything huge to them – just go be with them as a friend who is near and whose love can be felt by your physical presence.

CRYING OUT FOR GOD'S PRESENCE

Aim: To discover God's presence in the dry places

Having a fresh sense of God's presence is so important for a healthy spiritual life. But what do we do when our spiritual throats and mouths feel dry? Are there things we can do to get our souls drinking from God's streams of living water again?

Psalm 42 lets us into a world where God seems distant, where the closest David can get to God is the memory of days past. And yet he manages to find a way to drink in God's fresh presence again.

Read the passage together

> As the deer pants for streams of water,
> so my soul pants for you, O God.
> My soul thirsts for God, for the living God.
> When can I go and meet with God?
> My tears have been my food
> day and night,
> while men say to me all day long,
> "Where is your God?"
> These things I remember
> as I pour out my soul:
> how I used to go with the multitude,
> leading the procession to the house of God,
> with shouts of joy and thanksgiving
> among the festive throng.
>
> Why are you downcast, O my soul?
> Why so disturbed within me?
> Put your hope in God,
> for I will yet praise him,
> my Saviour and my God.

My soul is downcast within me;
therefore I will remember you
from the land of the Jordan,
the heights of Hermon—from Mount Mizar.
Deep calls to deep
in the roar of your waterfalls;
all your waves and breakers
have swept over me.

By day the LORD directs his love,
at night his song is with me—
a prayer to the God of my life.

I say to God my Rock,
"Why have you forgotten me?
Why must I go about mourning,
oppressed by the enemy?"
My bones suffer mortal agony
as my foes taunt me,
saying to me all day long,
"Where is your God?"

Why are you downcast, O my soul?
Why so disturbed within me?
Put your hope in God,
for I will yet praise him,
my Saviour and my God.

Psalm 42

TO SET THE SCENE

Draw a picture that symbolises how near you feel to God at the moment. Show your picture to the group and be prepared to share how your drawing demonstrates your feelings.

HOW DOES THIS **APPLY TO ME**

1. David compares his desire to experience God afresh to that of a thirsty deer drinking by a bubbling stream. How thirsty would you say you are? How fresh is your spiritual drinking water?

2. David speaks about going to a place to meet with God. How important is it for you to have a place to meet with God? Do you find it easier to experience God in a church or in your own private space? What are the pros or cons of each?

3. How does keeping your relationship with God fresh help you to be a 'living testimony of God's love' to those around you? Should you always expect your faith to be appreciated by others?

4. Read Hebrews 10:25. How important is public worship, going to church regularly, in the life of a Christian? Do you think church attendance helps or hinders your faith? Why?

WHAT DOES SEARCH THE BIBLE SAY?
5. What do you think David means here when he says to his soul in verse 5, 'Put your hope in God'? What are some real ways you can also place your hope in God that may help you sense his nearness again? Let Hebrews 11:1 give you some ideas.

6. Think back over your life as a Christian. Are there times you can remember when God felt especially close? Were you doing anything during those times to cultivate that intimacy with God? What can you learn from those times?

7. What are the things you find repeatedly washing into your life and taking away the sense of God's nearness? What are some practical ways for you to overcome those distractions and allow God's presence to wash over you instead?

8. Look over this psalm. How did David renew his experience of God's fresh presence?

9. Have you ever felt forgotten by God or by other fellow believers? What are some ways to help fight the 'spiritual blues' we all face from time to time?

HOW DOES THIS APPLY TO ME
10. What new spiritual discipline might help you draw nearer to God each day? Would it vary? Can you try to put it into practice?

WORSHIP

Take a few minutes to be still before God, remembering times in the past when you have felt him near and heard his still small voice. Thank him for those times. Now break into pairs and quietly share things you could do to improve your spiritual life. Then pray for one another that God would help you to put those 'ways' into practice. Pray too for a fresh sense of God's presence for one another.

DURING THE WEEK

Read 1 Kings 19:1–18. Consider whether you have experienced more of God in your life through his powerful wind, earthquake, fire – or his still small voice. Take a bit of time each day this week to read a psalm of your choice and sit quietly, listening out for God to speak to you in the silence. If it helps, keep a notepad and write down what you think he was saying to you that day.

Try implementing some or all of your answer to Question 10 as a daily routine.

CRYING OUT FOR COMFORT

Aim: To find our true source of comfort in the midst of all the world's troubles

If it's not one thing it's another. We are quite often surrounded by trouble and if our lives aren't being squeezed on all sides, then the lives of those we care about are. The world is filled with all kinds of trouble: wars, rumours of war, financial worries, personal crises – how can we find peace and comfort with so much bad news?

The psalmist tells us our source of comfort is found in God. He proclaims, 'God is our refuge and strength, an ever-present help in trouble.'

Read the passage together

God is our refuge and strength,
an ever-present help in trouble.
Therefore we will not fear, though the earth give way
and the mountains fall into the heart of the sea,
though its waters roar and foam and the mountains quake with their surging.

There is a river whose streams make glad the city of God,
the holy place where the Most High dwells.
God is within her, she will not fall;
God will help her at break of day.
Nations are in uproar, kingdoms fall;
he lifts his voice, the earth melts.

The LORD Almighty is with us;
the God of Jacob is our fortress.

Come and see the works of the LORD,
the desolations he has brought on the earth.
He makes wars cease to the ends of the earth;
he breaks the bow and shatters the spear,
he burns the shields with fire.

"Be still, and know that I am God;
I will be exalted among the nations,
I will be exalted in the earth."

The LORD Almighty is with us;
the God of Jacob is our fortress.
Selah

Psalm 46

TO SET THE SCENE

What brings you comfort when you feel stressed? Is it eating chocolate? Spending money? Talking to friends? Going for a drive? Playing sport? Praying? Take a few minutes to think about your answer and share it with the group.

DID YOU KNOW?

Like Psalm 42, this psalm is credited to the sons of Korah. This passage seems to have no specific historical setting. This is a hymn that focuses the worshipper on the refuge and protection of God.

Martin Luther used Psalm 46 as the basis of his famous hymn *A mighty fortress is our God*. The psalm certainly demonstrates that no matter what force opposes God or his people, God will easily prevail and so we can find our comfort in trusting him.

HOW DOES THIS

APPLY TO ME

1. The psalmist proclaims that 'God is our refuge and strength, an ever-present help in trouble.' What kind of troubles do you most often face in your life? And what means of coping have you found helpful?

2. Can you think of practical things you can do to discover more and more of God as a source of comfort for you? Are there ways you can think of that will allow God to be a real helper when trouble comes?

3. Verses 2 and 3 seem to picture the end of the world. Some local Christians used this psalm in Pakistan after a cataclysmic earthquake. It was sung as a witness of God's readiness to help, even in terrible catastrophe. How would you cope if you were faced with a similar calamity? Do these verses offer any comfort to you in your life situation? How?

WHAT DOES **SEARCH** **THE BIBLE SAY?** **4.** Read Revelation 21:1–7. When you imagine the future kingdom of God, as described in both Revelation 21 and verses 4–7 of this psalm, what does it look like and how will it feel? How can you draw comfort now from knowing the world will one day be as described in these scriptures?

5. When trouble comes, it is sometimes easy to fall into the trap of not knowing who will prevail – God or evil. How much more powerful do you think God is than evil? How can knowing the difference help keep you from despair?

6. How much do you see God as a help in your daily life? As you look back over the course of your life, describe from today's perspective how God may have been there for you even when you couldn't sense his presence. How did he help you then and how can knowing that help you now?

7. If God really is our 'fortress,' what practical ways can you think of to hide behind his walls and take refuge in his protection?

8. In verse 8 we are exhorted to 'come see the works of the Lord.' What do you think are the works of God? How will 'seeing them' help us? In what ways can we see them?

9. Look through this psalm and as a group call out all the words that describe God and what he offers us as his people. Since we know these are true, what can you do to experience them deep down when life feels full of turmoil?

10. What are some habits you can develop that will help to build an ongoing sense of God's help and comfort?

WORSHIP

Have some current headlines written out on paper or cut out of the newspaper and take time to pray for those who are facing disaster from natural causes or war or through other suffering, caused by the sinful way we treat one another. Ask God to overrule in those situations and then ask him to rule in your own lives too. Pray for his kingdom to come soon (Rev. 22:20).

DURING THE WEEK

Take time each day to sit, be still and read Psalm 46. As you read and meditate, take time to remember ways God has been faithful to you in the past and ask for him to continue to direct your path in his ways of peace. End your prayer time with the Lord's Prayer – especially asking that 'his kingdom come and his will be done on earth as it is in heaven.'

CRYING OUT FOR FORGIVENESS

AIM

Aim: To discover God's forgiveness as we are penitent before him

What do we do when we really mess things up? When we sin, even in the worst possible ways, can we really know and experience God's forgiveness? Is it possible to truly move on in the promise of a future with God?

Psalm 51 is a heart cry to God for forgiveness. 'Create in me a pure heart, O God' is a cry to be made new again – a cry not only for forgiveness, but for re-creation, restoration, even re-birth. This psalm offers hope to all who want to experience a fresh, clean start through God's redeeming power.

Read the passage together

> *Have mercy on me, O God,*
> *according to your unfailing love;*
> *according to your great compassion*
> *blot out my transgressions.*
> *Wash away all my iniquity*
> *and cleanse me from my sin.*
>
> *For I know my transgressions,*
> *and my sin is always before me.*
> *Against you, you only, have I sinned*
> *and done what is evil in your sight,*
> *so that you are proved right when you speak*
> *and justified when you judge.*
> *Surely I was sinful at birth,*
> *sinful from the time my mother conceived me.*
> *Surely you desire truth in the inner parts;*
> *you teach me wisdom in the inmost place.*

Cleanse me with hyssop, and I will be clean;
wash me, and I will be whiter than snow.
Let me hear joy and gladness;
let the bones you have crushed rejoice.
Hide your face from my sins
and blot out all my iniquity.

Create in me a pure heart, O God,
and renew a steadfast spirit within me.
Do not cast me from your presence
or take your Holy Spirit from me.
Restore to me the joy of your salvation
and grant me a willing spirit, to sustain me.

Then I will teach transgressors your ways,
and sinners will turn back to you.
Save me from bloodguilt, O God,
the God who saves me,
and my tongue will sing of your righteousness.
O Lord, open my lips,
and my mouth will declare your praise.
You do not delight in sacrifice, or I would bring it;
you do not take pleasure in burnt offerings.
The sacrifices of God are a broken spirit;
a broken and contrite heart,
O God, you will not despise.

In your good pleasure make Zion prosper;
build up the walls of Jerusalem.
Then there will be righteous sacrifices,
whole burnt offerings to delight you;
then bulls will be offered on your altar.

Psalm 51

TO SET THE SCENE

Break into twos. Give each pair a newspaper and ask them to identify stories where forgiveness is needed. Ask them to tear out the relevant stories and place them in order of which situations they would find harder to forgive. Have each team share the story headlines and why they thought they were harder or easier to forgive.

DID YOU KNOW?

Psalm 51 is set in the context of terrible sin. David had recently coveted Bath-sheba and committed adultery with her. He then murdered her husband, thus effectively enabling himself to steal another man's wife. Finally, as he married Bathsheba, he lived a lie before all of Israel. David, king of Israel, broke at least five of the Ten Commandments in this one incident.

According to the law, the sins of adultery and murder carried a higher penalty than lying, stealing or coveting. The law called for David's execution. And yet, even in this story, we see a life taken for a life. As a direct result of his sin, David loses his son, the result of his tryst with Bathsheba, while he is forgiven and goes free.

The loss of his son was not all that David suffered as a result of his sin. But there is an interesting correlation between the loss of David's son as a result of his sin, and the sacrifice of David's greater son, Jesus, so that we may all know God's forgiveness.

1. What kind of sin committed against you would you find most difficult to forgive? Would you be able to forgive? When you think of evil men like Hitler, Stalin or Pol Pot, do you think it would ever be possible for God to forgive their sins?

HOW DOES THIS **2.** When you sin do you feel you have done enough in confessing it to God and accepting his forgiveness? Do you some-
APPLY TO ME times feel you have to punish yourself in some way or do some act of kindness or charity to make up for your wrong? Why do you think we natu-rally feel we must do good to counteract the wrong things we do?

3. What was the basis on which David appealed to God for forgiveness of his sin?

4. Sin takes its toll on us by making us feel inwardly stained and separated from God – all alone. Have you ever felt this way, and if so how did you deal with it? In what ways is the need for personal purity expressed in this psalm?

5. In verse 5 David says, 'Surely I was sinful at birth, sinful from the time my mother conceived me.' Does this mean we sin because we are born sinners? If that is the case, in what ways can you find hope in this passage and in the New Testament?

6. Read verse 4. In the Lord's Prayer we pray, 'Forgive us our sins as we forgive those who sin against us.' In the light of these two scriptures, why do you think it is important for us to forgive those who sin against us? You may want to read Matthew 18:21–35 for further insight.

7. Read 2 Samuel 12:1-25. Do you think David was a better king as a result of the incidents that took place around this psalm? Why?

8. There are times in life when God allows us, like David, to be in circumstances where we end up broken before him. Has this ever happened to you? If so, what did you learn from it? Have those times made you better or worse off? How?

9. David understood he was broken and helpless before God. He couldn't fix the great mess he had created. How much do you rely on your own strength to try and fix things and make them right and how much do you trust God? Are there any Bible passages you can think of that remind you of how committed God is to seeing your life restored to his will?

10. Looking at this psalm, what can you see as some of the results of experiencing God's forgiveness?

WORSHIP

Pray the Lord's Prayer together as a group – taking a minute to pause after the 'forgive us our sins' section. In the pause try to think through those you may be having a hard time forgiving. Seek to offer them to God and ask him for his help and strength as you seek the choice of forgiveness. Close the time of prayer by finishing the Lord's Prayer and then offer prayers of thanks to God for forgiveness of your own sin and his promise to give you a clean heart.

DURING THE WEEK

Take time each day to be quiet before God and pray Psalm 51 to him. In the quiet, remember your forgiveness is not based on the good you do to make up for the wrongs you commit. It is based on God's love and compassion.

CRYING OUT IN THANKS AND PRAISE

Aim: To take account of all God has done for us and to remember to thank and praise him

How often do we forget to say 'thank you' when we are helped or to compliment someone who has been there for us? Yet we expect it when we are supportive or helpful to others and feel hurt when it doesn't come.

Our memories can be so short. God has done so much for us and yet it is so easy to forget to thank and praise him. Where would we be without him and his committed love, compassion and saving help? Remembering all that God has done for us and thanking and praising him are so important!

Read the passage together

Praise the LORD, O my soul;
all my inmost being, praise his holy name.
Praise the LORD, O my soul,
and forget not all his benefits-
who forgives all your sins
and heals all your diseases,
who redeems your life from the pit
and crowns you with love and compassion,
who satisfies your desires with good things
so that your youth is renewed like the eagle's.

The LORD works righteousness
and justice for all the oppressed.

He made known his ways to Moses,
his deeds to the people of Israel:
The LORD is compassionate and gracious,
slow to anger, abounding in love.
He will not always accuse,
nor will he harbour his anger forever;

he does not treat us as our sins deserve
or repay us according to our iniquities.
For as high as the heavens are above the earth,
so great is his love for those who fear him;
as far as the east is from the west,
so far has he removed our transgressions from us.
As a father has compassion on his children,
so the LORD has compassion on those who fear him;
for he knows how we are formed,
he remembers that we are dust.
As for man, his days are like grass,
he flourishes like a flower of the field;
the wind blows over it and it is gone,
and its place remembers it no more.
But from everlasting to everlasting
the LORD's love is with those who fear him,
and his righteousness with their children's children–
with those who keep his covenant
and remember to obey his precepts.

The LORD has established his throne in heaven,
and his kingdom rules over all.
Praise the LORD, you his angels,
you mighty ones who do his bidding,
who obey his word.
Praise the LORD, all his heavenly hosts,
you his servants who do his will. Praise the LORD, all his works
everywhere in his dominion.

Praise the LORD, O my soul.

Psalm 103:1–22

TO SET THE SCENE

Take a pen and paper and give yourself three minutes to write a 'Thanks and Praise' list of the things you are thankful to God for. Now share appropriate parts of your list with the rest of the group. Did what others shared spark any other things you are thankful for? Write those down as well.

Psalm 103 opens a section of psalms of praise – from 103 to 107 – but is thought to be part of a pair with Psalm 104. It is attributed to David but was also used extensively by Israel when in exile in Babylon. It is a hymn sung by an individual first from his own heart to God and then on behalf of the rest of the congregation.

Henry Francis Lyte used this hymn as the basis for his famous hymn *Praise, my soul, the King of heaven,* which was sung at the wedding of Queen Elizabeth II.

Psalm 103 is appropriate both for the calamity of exile and when facing the demands of a very public royal marriage. In both instances – as for the rest of human life – this psalm reminds us God not only knows us in our frailty, fallenness and weakness but, despite this will redeem us, uphold us and deliver us to eternal life – bless his holy name!

1. In the context of this psalm, what do you see as the difference between praise and thanks?

2. Look through this psalm and list the reasons David gives us to praise God here.

HOW DOES THIS / APPLY TO ME

3. The Hebrew word used for 'praise' in the opening and closing verses of this psalm also means 'bless' as in 'bless the Lord, oh my soul.' In this passage David has to bless God from his deepest parts (soul – inmost being) because of what the Lord has done for him. Can you remember a time when you felt so grateful to God that you felt you would burst if you didn't 'bless' him? Share that memory.

4. Verses 9–18 speak of God's committed love towards us in the face of our weakness and sinfulness. Using these verses, how would you describe God's love? How do these words about God's love make you feel? Why?

5. Verse 14 tells us God 'knows how we are formed, he remembers that we are dust.' Some would say this statement is telling us God knows and accepts our limits, even when we do not. What does this verse say to you? How do you think this is meant to encourage us?

WHAT DOES

SEARCH

THE BIBLE SAY?

6. Verses 7–8 refer to God's faithfulness despite Israel's gross sin of idol worship at Mt. Sinai. Verse 8 is almost a direct quote of Exodus 34:6. Read Exodus 34:1–10 and discuss why you think David would refer to it here.

WHAT DOES

SEARCH

THE BIBLE SAY?

7. Verses 15–17 speak of the shortness of our life in contrast to the everlasting nature of God's love. Compare this to Matthew 6:25–35. What reason do these verses give you to thank and praise God?

HOW DOES THIS

?

APPLY TO ME

8. This psalm starts with a single worshipper praising and thanking God from the depths of his being. But it rises in a crescendo through all of God's people, to his angels, 'mighty ones,' heavenly hosts, servants, and finally to 'all his works everywhere in his dominion.' Why do you think all of creation should thank and praise God? How does this encourage you in your worship of God?

9. What benefits do you think we gain from praising and thanking God?

10. Today you created a 'Thanks and Praise' list. Can you help others in your group think of any other creative ways to thank and praise God in their daily lives?

WORSHIP

Look through your 'Thanks and Praise' list. Take a few minutes to thank God and praise him by using statements from your list. End your time of prayer with a praise song you can sing together, with or without music.

DURING THE WEEK

Take the 'Thanks and Praise' list home with you. Take a few minutes each day to see if there is anything you can think of to add to the list. Then offer thanks and praise to God for all he has done for you. Use your own method for remembering and praising if you like.

LEADERS' GUIDE

TO HELP YOU LEAD

You may have led a group many times before or this may be your first time. Here is some advice on how to lead these studies:

▶ As a group leader, you don't have to be an expert or a lecturer. You are there to facilitate the learning of the group members – helping them to discover for themselves the wisdom in God's word. You should not be doing most of the talking or dishing out the answers, whatever the group expects of you!

▶ You do need to be aware of the group's dynamics, however. People can be quite quick to label themselves and each other in a group situation. One person might be seen as the expert, another the moaner who always has something to complain about. One person may be labelled as quiet and not be expected to contribute; another person may always jump in with something to say. Be aware of the different types of individuals in the group, but don't allow the labels to stick. You may need to encourage those who find it hard to get a word in, and quieten down those who always have something to say. Talk to members between sessions to find out how they feel about the group.

▶ The sessions are planned to try to engage every member in actively learning. Of course you cannot force anyone to take part if they don't want to, but it won't be too easy to be a spectator. Activities that ask everyone to write something down, or to talk in twos and then report back to the group, are there for a reason. They give everyone space to think and form their opinion, even if not everyone voices it out loud.

▶ Do adapt the sessions for your group as you feel is appropriate. Some groups may know each other very well and will be prepared to talk at a deep level. New groups may take a bit of time to get to know each other before making themselves vulnerable, but encourage members to share their lives with each other.

▶ Encourage a number of replies to each question. The study is not about finding a single right answer, but about sharing experiences and thoughts in order to find out how to apply the Bible to people's lives. When brainstorming, don't be too quick to evaluate the contributions. Write everything down and then have a look to see which suggestions are worth keeping.

▶ Similarly encourage everyone to ask questions, to voice doubts and to discuss difficulties. Some parts of the Bible are hard to understand. Sometimes the Christian faith throws up paradoxes. Painful things happen to us that make it difficult to see what God is doing. A housegroup should be a safe place to express all this. If discussion doesn't resolve the issue, send everyone away to pray about it, and ask you minister for advice!

▶ Give yourself time in the week to read through the Bible passage and the questions. Read the Leaders' notes for the session, as different ways of presenting the questions are sometimes suggested. However, during the session, don't be too quick to come in with the answer – sometimes we need space to think.

▶ Delegate as much as you like! The easiest activities to delegate are reading the text and the worship suggestions, but there are other ways to involve the group members. Giving people responsibility can help them own the session much more.

▶ Pray for group members by name, that God would meet with them during the week. Pray for the group session that it will be a constructive and helpful time. Ask the Lord to equip you as you lead the group.

THE STRUCTURE OF EACH SESSION

Feedback: find out what people remember from the previous session and if they have been able to act during the week on what was discussed last time.

To set the scene: an activity or a question to get everyone thinking about the subject to be studied.

Bible reading: it's important actually to read the passage you are studying during the session. Ask someone to prepare this in advance or go around the group reading a verse or two each. But don't assume everyone will be happy to read out loud.

Questions and activities: these are designed to promote discussion on how to apply what the passage says to your individual/group situation.

During the week: a specific task to do during the week to help people put into practice what they have learned.

Prayer: suggestions for creative prayer. Use these suggestions alongside other group expressions of worship such as singing. Add a prayer time with opportunities to pray for group members and their families and friends.

GROUND RULES

How do people know what is expected of them during your meetings? Is it ever discussed, or do they just pick up clues from each other? You may find it helpful to discuss some ground rules for the housegroup at the start of this course, even if your group has been going a long time. This also gives you an opportunity to talk about how you, as the leader, see the group. Ask everyone to think about what they want to get out of the course. How do they want the group to work? What values do they want to be part of the group's experience: honesty, respect, confidentiality?

How do they want their contributions to be treated? You could ask everyone to write down three ground rules on slips of paper and put them in a bowl. Pass the bowl around the group. Each person takes out a rule and reads it, and someone collates the list. Discuss the ground rules that have been suggested and come up with a top five. This method enables everyone to contribute fairly anonymously. Alternatively, if your group are all quite vocal, have a straight discussion about it!

ICONS

The aim of the session

Engaging with the world

Investigate what else the Bible says

How does this apply to me?

What about my church?

NB not all questions in each session are covered, some are self-explanatory

SESSION 1

MATERIALS NEEDED

A slip of paper and pen for each person in the group.
A hat or bowl to hold the slips.
Some candles or soft light.
A quiet piece of instrumental music that can be played in the background.

1. There does seem to be a progression in verse 1. First there is the occasional falling into the thought patterns of the world. Then there is a more enduring relationship with attitudes and behaviours that take us further from God. This is 'standing' with those who are unconcerned about eradicating sin from their lives. Finally, there is the act of being 'seated' in a camp that places us firmly apart from God and his ways that impart true peace and happiness.

2. Understanding what is meant by 'the law' here is important. The psalms never mean 'the Law' as in the five books of Moses. 'The law' means knowing God and his ways. For us that includes knowing Jesus as the Lord God and taking the time and patience to learn his commands.

3. By taking the time to develop a personal relationship with Jesus through Bible study and prayer and by emulating his life, we will come to know God and true happiness. Get the group to see that meditation needn't be something just for mystics and monks – help them see it as something as simple as memorising a Bible verse, or reflecting on their life in light of a scripture, or rereading the same Bible passage at set times throughout a given day. Ask the group if they can come up with some creative ways to engage deeper with God's Word.

4. It is important to be honest and allow the group to compare the lifestyle of their friends to their own. At first glance we may think those we know are better off than ourselves and therefore more happy. Living in such a consumer-culture, it is often easy to forget that true inner happiness, peace and joy is not attained through 'stuff' but rather in whom we know. The more your group thinks about the quality of life their most well-off friends enjoy, the more they may begin to notice the cracks that betray a deeper longing for the inner substance and stability of a relationship with Christ.

5. For some, knowing that God is so intimately involved in their lives will bring comfort. For others there may be fear – especially of getting out of God's 'perfect will.' Be careful to emphasise that the object of this psalm is knowing God and experiencing his joy in all its fullness, rather than 'getting it all right.'

6. It is so easy to be critical and place the blame of failure on others so far away from us that, by implication, we absolve ourselves. It is important to note we all fail to keep God's law before us 'day and night' and live it out before the rest of the world. Seeking to find practical ways to put a love of God's law into action will help empower members of your group to move from wallowing in failures to moving positively towards real change through action.

7. Jesus' blessings reveal that true happiness does not come through experiencing a life without problems. In fact, as followers of Jesus we will have more than our fair share! What Jesus and the psalmist are saying is that we will experience true happiness by knowing God and living his way rather than the way of the world.

8. It is important to note that as we grow deeper in our relationship with God and learn and live his law, God will be directing our way towards making a difference in the lives of others. God gave Israel the law so that others would also come to know his wisdom and goodness (Deut. 4:5–8). Our happiness should be the thing that other people see in us and want for themselves.

WORSHIP

Give everybody time and space to reflect on this image. You may need to dim the lights, have some soft instrumental music playing and have a few candles lit to set the atmosphere. You may want to ask everyone to close their eyes and then slowly read the questions. Once you come to the very end of this worship time, pray a prayer that encourages those present not to focus on self-condemnation, but rather the hope we have in God who is committed to conforming us into the image of Christ (Rom. 8:29) – deeply rooting us in himself.

DURING THE WEEK

Encourage your group not to be fearful about being salt and light. This is an exercise of praying for others and being mindful of how we reflect God's blessing to others. Discuss ways of sharing which are not overt – perhaps by showing kindness by serving someone or giving them a book or inviting them for a meal or to a service in your church (if it's relevant).

SESSION 2

MATERIALS NEEDED

Paper and pen.

Optional: some candles or soft light; a quiet piece of instrumental music that can be played in the background for the final worship section

1. This is a simple exercise designed to give your group members an overall feel for this psalm. Help the group to note how positive God's love and commitment are to his people – right from making us to knowing us and exercising his sovereign right to govern us.

2. Note how God is declared faithful and full of unfailing love in the context of the earth and its creation. See if anyone notices how many times the phrase 'unfailing love' is used in the whole of this psalm.

3. In the context of this verse fear is the same thing as reverence. In this psalm reverence is generated by understanding God's faithful love in the face of humanity's rejection of him and his ways. In light of human rebellion, God's loving-kindness towards us is nothing short of awesome.

4. It is easy to think these verses are speaking more generally of God's working throughout human history. It is difficult for us to grasp that we are a part of 'the plans of the nations' and 'the purposes of the peoples.' In fact, even through the difficulties we face through our daily living, God is still working out his plans and purposes.

5. You may want to have someone practice reading this passage dramatically ahead of time. Or, you could have the group read it in a round. Some parallels can be seen in God accomplishing his will in our lives and his loving commitment to do so. He has ensured this through the offering up of his Son. Paul does not equate God being for us and committed to us with us having easy lives. In fact, Paul intimates the opposite here; and yet God will accomplish his ultimate plan to make us like Jesus and bring us to his kingdom.

6. It is easy to despair about the state of the church in connection with God's will. It is also easy to see the church as 'them.' Get the group to see that they are the church and think of practical ways they can demonstrate God's love to those around them.

7. In verses 13–15 the word 'all' is repeated three times – once in each verse. This is a poetical emphasis on the fact that, unlike humans, God sees all and understands every single human heart. God discerns and untangles the human heart like no other.

8. Remember what 'fear' means in our relationship with God and re-emphasise how that relates to God's love for us. It is in God's unfailing love that we are called to hope (rest).

9. In verses 20 and 21 the words 'wait' and 'trust' go hand in hand with 'hope' and 'rejoice.' We can only experience one because we do the other. It is as we trust God and rest in him that we can truly begin to surrender ourselves enough to him to allow the Spirit to manifest his fruit in our lives.

10. Both the recurrent theme and underlying reason for praise and hope in this psalm is God's loving-kindness – his unfailing love. God has made us in love, guided us in love and will deliver us into his unfailing love. We hope in him because we know he will accomplish his will of showing his love to us and the whole earth.

WORSHIP

Use this exercise as a meditation. You may want to choose music or be very quiet. Close the time with a quiet but firm reading of Psalm 33.

SESSION 3

YOU WILL NEED

A blindfold for each person.
A pen and paper for each person.

1. It is interesting to take note of what members of your group feel they are being saved from... or to. This question is designed to help give the group a broader view of the psalm and to see the wide spectrum of answers available.

2. Get the group to answer from their own thinking first. Use both verse 1 and Lamentations 3:22–23 to help them understand God's ongoing commitment to our daily salvation. That new song is not just for us, but for everyone.

3. Our salvation is meant to spread so that our whole community is affected, which should in turn affect all of the earth. Proclamation and declaration are important – not just in words, but also through helping people understand why we are what we are and do what we do. Does the group see any difference between the two? Help everyone feel there is a mutual accountability available for being a witness both locally and globally.

4. What we believe others feel about us colours our view of them. Believing God is waiting for us to step out line so he can hit us, or is unconcerned with how we live our lives, is not beneficial for us to come to a deep life-changing under-standing of his committed love. Knowing God's loving commitment to deliver us safely to his kingdom should give us a healthy reverence for him – because of his power to save. And it should cause us to praise him!

5. There is so much that competes with God and his work in our lives on a daily basis. In many cases there are also other 'isms' or thought systems that do not match up with whom the Bible says we are to trust in for our salvation. They are 'useless' in saving us. Let the group identify those things that are the 'little gods' in their lives.

6. These verses make it clear that there is only one God. He is the only one who can save, all the rest are pretenders. Jesus makes this plain in his own words too.

Although we should always show love and respect to those of other faiths, it is okay to want to share Jesus' claims with them. Encourage members of your group to learn about other faiths and to be resourced in sharing the good news with others. Perhaps different group members can take responsibility for a particular faith and then bringing that back to the group as a whole.

There are a lot of helpful free resources on the internet. A good place to start is the Church Mission Society website at: www.cms-uk.org.

7. God's salvation is for the whole earth. It is eagerly longed for by all of creation because the world is not all that it should/will be. When all things are transformed by God's glory, the whole creation will worship him eternally.

8. A natural result of our salvation is gratitude and adoration of the one who saved us. Israel's offerings were grain and animals, the same as our offerings of time and money. While any form of giving can bring glory to God, it is important that a good part of our offering of time and money goes to spreading God's message of salvation so all can hear and believe.

Help the group to see past giving as simply sending money. Help them see their part in God's grand plan of salvation sharing – both locally and globally. Get the group to come up with some practical ideas.

SESSION 4

MATERIALS NEEDED

None, but it might be a good idea to find out up-to-date situations for anyone in or connected with the church who has been having a difficult time recently.

1. In verses 1–5 there is a contradiction for the psalmist. He knows that God was close to his fathers – they trusted (used three times here for emphasis) in God and were delivered. But that is not how he feels right now.

3. In verses 9–11, David consoles himself by remembering the times when God was faithful to him – casting his mind back even to his birth. God is no casual friend but rather has a personal lifelong care for David.

4. In verse 11 David makes it clear that he is not looking for healing or deliverance from his troubles. What he wants is to know God's closeness again – in fact, this is his complaint in verse 1 as well. David feels he could face death or sickness squarely if God were there as his helper.

6. These verses call on everyone to praise God because he does not despise those who are suffering or afflicted. Verse 24 reminds us that God does listen and respond, even when we are unaware of it. Verse 26 tells us God is on the side of the poor and will satisfy them and any others who truly seek, no matter what the circumstances. Matthew 7:7–12 clarifies this in Jesus' own words.

7. God is all powerful and will stop the evil that causes us suffering. But God is also all loving and so he delays his return in order to give more time for evil people to turn to him before final judgement. When we ask God to intervene in the evil we see in the world and put a stop to it, we are also asking him to intervene in our own lives and stop us in our evil too. One day he will: verses 26–29 give us a glimpse of the future when Christ will reign and all evil and suffering will cease. Until then we can take comfort from the fact that God intimately knows our suffering: he experienced it as God the Son, rejected both by humanity and by God the Father, and in that suffering has provided a way for all to escape the judgement we deserve.

8. If we can develop a perspective of God as the one who loves us with everlasting commitment and will deliver us, as one who will certainly accomplish his will over all, and keep that perspective set in our hearts, then no matter what, we will have hope and strength, even in the midst of extreme trials and suffering. Read 2 Corinthians 4:7–12 for further insight.

SESSION 5

MATERIALS NEEDED
Paper and pen for each person in the group.

1. How much we drink is directly linked to how thirsty we feel. Discuss how often you feel you need to commune with God in order to feel you are growing in your relationship and experience of God's presence.

2. There is a place for both public and private worship in the balanced Christian life. Help the group to see the need for both. Sharing one another's experiences may help people try out new ways of developing their spiritual lives.

3. There is a direct relationship between experiencing God and others seeing his 'shine' on our faces. However, others do not always respond well to our own inner joy. We need then to remember God is the source of our happiness, not acceptance by others.

4. Our experience of faith is meant to be shared as a body of believers. In order to know a full sense of God's presence we must be in fellowship with a gathering of God's people. Corporate worship has always been an important part of experiencing God's fullness – even in David's day – and especially now as we are all part of the body of Christ. Hebrews tells us to meet together in order to encourage each other.

5. If 'faith is being sure of what we hope for and certain of what we do not see' then having a faith based on an experience of God is very important. The writer of Hebrews cultivates faith by remembering what God has done in the lives of other believers (Chapter 11). Like the psalmist, the group may be able to do the same by remembering how God has been faithful in their own lives.

6. Quite often we experience spiritual drought because of sins we've committed or things we have failed to do. We need to weigh up our lives honestly to see if God's presence is being choked out or not sought out.

7. We can be washed out by all the troubles and cares that come our way or we can develop a focus and confidence in God that helps us become those who overcome. Help the group to find ways to keep their hearts centred on God – even in the midst of problems. This may even be by relying on one another for mutual encouragement.

8. David renewed his experience of God's fresh presence by: admitting his need for God (v1), looking for ways to feed his soul's thirst (v2), not dwelling on those people or situations which get in the way of knowing God's presence (vv3, 9–10), taking time to remember past experiences of God and learning from those (vv4–6), worshipping corporately (v4), making the effort to praise and worship God (vv4–5, 11), singing and praying to God (v8), self-examination in the light of God's truth (v11).

9. Remember we are all in this together. Our spiritual well-being is a group responsibility. We need to care for one another and we must also not be too proud to ask for help for when we need it.

10. Be creative here. Different people will have different ideas that perhaps others will never have heard of. Allow people to share how their differing disciplines have helped their spiritual life. Encourage experimentation and to make this exercise more than just ideas. Put them into practice. You may find Ian McDowall's *Christ the Bodybuilder*[1] or Richard Foster's *Celebration of discipline*[2] helpful.

---

1 Ian McDowall, *Christ the Bodybuilder*, (Milton Keynes: Authentic, 2004)
2 Richard Foster, *Celebration of discipline*, (London: Hodder & Stoughton, 1998)

SESSION 6

MATERIALS NEEDED

Newspaper headlines, or pieces of paper with current catastrophes and world problems written on them.

2. We can take refuge in acknowledging that God knows all things rather than trusting in our own limited knowledge. By believing God is in control of all the affairs of humanity, we can rest in him, knowing he will bring things to a right conclusion.

4. This is a good opportunity to dream of the future as a group. Take a little while to create hope – we can take comfort in all that these two passages promise will come to pass. Spend a few minutes in God's promised future for us and experience how encouraging that is. It is a great way to start each day, focussed on where we are going and God's commitment to get us there!

5. Verse 6 shows us that with just a word from God the earth melts. We do not live in a world where God's power struggles against the strength of evil. God has a plan and he will accomplish it at the right time.

6. Taking note of God's faithfulness to us in past time generates hope and trust in him now.

7. Be creative. Reading the Bible and praying are great ways to find encouragement or refuge in God as we are reminded of his attributes, but what about hearing someone else's testimony, reading some church history or a missionary's story? How about meditating on God's attributes?

8. The works of the Lord in this context are the ways God has helped us in the past – in the Bible, church history and our lives, and the wonders of creation. Meditate on God's future plans and how we will experience those and how God's return and rule will affect all creation.

9. This psalm tells us that, no matter what, God is there for us as a refuge, a strength, a ready help, a city of refuge and a fortress. The psalmist intimates that even when there is calamity around us, if (v10) we simply still ourselves and focus on God and his attributes mentioned here, we will find comfort and know his peace in the storm.

SESSION 7

MATERIALS NEEDED

Some daily newspapers.

1. We find it fairly easy to forgive people for minor sins, and despite the excruciating pain of cases of extreme betrayal, like adultery, we can still move on over time – and even bring ourselves to forgive those who have hurt us so deeply. But what about the most evil of people – can they too be forgiven if they cry out to God for forgiveness in repentance for their evil deeds?

2. We naturally tend to want to do good in order to right past wrongs – to 'tip the scales in our favour.' Although we should seek to compensate those for the harm we have caused them, it is wrong to see this as the basis for our forgiveness before a holy God who has already provided our means of forgiveness through the death of his Son, Jesus.

3. David was the king and could have been haughty and felt he did not need to answer to anyone for his actions. But he didn't. He knew he was guilty. His appeal for forgiveness was based on God's character – his unfailing love and compassion – and his grace.

4. David appeals to be washed and cleansed in verse 2. In verse 7 he asks to be purified with hyssop (an Old Testament reference to the hyssop branch used in purification rituals – Lev.14:48–53) and to be made whiter than snow. In verse 9 he asks God to hide his face from his sins and to blot out or remove all his iniquities. And in verse 10 he asks God to remake his heart so it will be pure.

5. There is no need for fatalism. These verses show David's basis for hope is not in humanity's lost-ness, which is a reality, but in the fact that God's 'mercy triumphs over judgement!' (James 2:13). God knows us and is committed to restoring those who cry out to him as David did.

6. When we sin, it is first and foremost against God – who chooses to forgive us. Therefore, how can we expect God to forgive us if we are unwilling to forgive those who have sinned against us?

9. In a very real way we need to 'let go and let God.' In resting in him and trusting him we will see him work as we allow his Holy Spirit control of our lives. Ultimately we can take comfort in the words of Paul in Philippians 1:6: 'He who began a good work in you will carry it on to completion until the day of Christ Jesus.' A lot of what we 'do' needs to be focussed on what God is currently doing in our own hearts and lives and trusting him for the final outcome.

10. Some of the results of experiencing God's forgiveness in Psalm 51 are encountering God's mercy, unfailing love, great compassion and delight (v1, v19); being cleansed and renewed (v2, v10); having guilt removed (v3, v7); knowing God's truth and wisdom (v6); experiencing joy, gladness, rejoicing and singing (v8, v12, v14); being able to share God's goodness with others (v13, v15); and having a hope for an eternal future with God (v18).

SESSION 8

MATERIALS NEEDED

Paper and pen.

Music for worship, if desired.

1. Praise is speaking to God in words of admiration or appreciation for who he is and what he does. Thanks is an expression of gratitude to God for a benefit received. So, in practical terms, 'praise' looks like 'God, you are full of compassion and mercy' while 'thanks' looks like 'Thank you God for your steadfast love.' We need to find ways of integrating both into our daily lives.

2. We praise God because he forgives (vv3, 12), heals (v3), redeems (v4), 'crowns' or adopts us as one of his royal family (v4), satisfies (v5), renews (v6), acts on behalf of the oppressed (v6), makes his ways and deeds known (v7), is compassionate (vv8, 13), is gracious (v8), is patient (v8), full of love (vv8, 11), does not hold a grudge (v9), does not give us what we deserve (v10), truly knows us (v14), is eternally committed to us (v17), makes us righteous and (v17) rules over all in his excellencies.

4. Have the group especially focus on the picture language David uses to express God's love and commitment to forgive us our sin. Phrases such as 'as high as the heavens' or 'as far as the east is from the west' or 'as a father has compassion on his children' paint a beautiful picture that tells us so much about God's love and why we should praise him for it.

5. God's love for us is eternally consistent (v17) – God understands our weaknesses and limitations and yet loves us as members of his covenant people through faith in his Son (v18).

7. Israel's rejection of God at Mt. Sinai is a grave sin. The worship of the golden calf resulted in the destruction of the first set of stone tablets containing the Ten Commandments and the death of many Israelites. But God's love is long-suffering and his forgiveness is without end for those he is in covenant with. Exodus 34 is a real-life reminder that 'the LORD is compassionate and gracious, slow to anger, abounding in love'(v8). See if anyone notices God's heart desire for all to experience his awesome works (Ex. 34:10).

8. The obvious reason we thank God from these verses is because he provides. But how far does his provision go? By allowing each passage to shed light on the other, we see that truly trusting God's everlasting love for our life now, day by day, means we can also trust him for everlasting life in the future, by and by. Everlasting love from an eternal God means everlasting life for 'those who fear him'.